T0209318

Also by Brad Hauter:

The Invisible Game
Counter Terrorism

POKEY JR

Even Roosters
Get Second Chances

Brad Hauter

BALBOA.PRESS
A DIVISION OF HAY HOUSE

Balboa Press books may be ordered through booksellers or by contacting:

Balboa Press
A Division of Hay House
1663 Liberty Drive
Bloomington, IN 47403
www.balboapress.com
844-682-1282

Because of the dynamic nature of the Internet, any web addresses or
links contained in this book may have changed since publication and
may no longer be valid. The views expressed in this work are solely those
of the author and do not necessarily reflect the views of the publisher,
and the publisher hereby disclaims any responsibility for them.

The author of this book does not dispense medical advice or prescribe
the use of any technique as a form of treatment for physical, emotional,
or medical problems without the advice of a physician, either directly
or indirectly. The intent of the author is only to offer information
of a general nature to help you in your quest for emotional and
spiritual well-being. In the event you use any of the information in
this book for yourself, which is your constitutional right, the author
and the publisher assume no responsibility for your actions.

Any people depicted in stock imagery provided by Getty Images are
models, and such images are being used for illustrative purposes only.
Certain stock imagery © Getty Images.

Print information available on the last page.

ISBN: 978-1-9822-5179-6 (sc)
ISBN: 978-1-9822-5178-9 (hc)
ISBN: 978-1-9822-5177-2 (e)

Library of Congress Control Number: 2020913730

Balboa Press rev. date: 09/21/2020

Dedication

This book is dedicated to Pokey... She is Pokey Jr's mom and the matriarch of our chicken yard. Without her 'unique' genetics, we wouldn't have ever met a rooster like Pokey Jr.

Contents

Foreword

My family has been lucky enough to know Brad and the Hauter family for the last eleven years. First, as our son's collegiate soccer coach, then as a friend and finally as a business colleague.

He's a family guy – through and through.

He thinks deeply and cares greatly about causes and topics that engage him – the environment, human motivation and meaning, helping others achieve their dreams. Don't let his easy laughter and quick wit fool you, there's a lot going on behind that smile.

But it's not just talk and reflection, he also puts action, energy and time into issues and projects that he cares about. (For goodness sakes, he drove a riding lawn mower across the country not once, but twice, setting a Guinness World Record and raising money and awareness for Keep America Beautiful.)

Of course, there are other things Brad loves, too. Like animals, for instance. All animals. But, especially chickens. Brad dreamed of being a chicken keeper for *years*. When he and his family eventually moved to a small farm in Illinois, that dream came true.

Instantly, he became interested in their social structure, their language and their fascinating behaviors. Like many chicken keepers, his flock quickly grew. And before there was time to say "chicken math", he was incubating his first batch of eggs – including an egg from his favorite hen, Pokey. Out of that egg emerged a rooster named Pokey Jr. and a lifetime bond between the two.

This is Pokey Jr's story as observed by his buddy, Brad. Like any life story, it is filled with achievements and setbacks, relationship highs and lows and the struggle for purpose. And through it all, lies a friendship for the ages.

If you love animals, if you appreciate the search for meaning or enjoy a good friendship story... this book's for you!

—Davi Reynolds

Preface

This story kind of wrote itself as it played out in front of us moment by moment. From the start it was clear mom was different from the rest of the flock but it took longer to learn the quirkiness of Pokey Jr. Initially he started out very 'rooster like' as he took over, ran the chicken yard and attacked anyone who he thought was a threat to the flock.

Our bond began to grow when he was in trouble and I think choking on something. We found him semi-unresponsive, gasping for air and with his comb purple instead of it's normal bright red. Seeing it, we did what we had done, right or wrong, to our kids when they were choking… Turned them upside down and whacked them on their back. While we didn't see anything pop out he did take a big breath and his comb returned to red pretty quickly.

While he still ran up and was aggressive when I was in the chicken yard his 'attacks' were more like taps. I'm not saying he felt a connection to me since that moment but… it's possible. This may have set the table of trust for him to seek me out on other rooster 'issues' and may have been the spark that led to this book.

Acknowledgment

My friend Mary Novak who lent her talents in review and editing.

The most awesome members of the Coop Dreams Team, Davi Reynolds and Reid Sprenkel, for living the Pokey Jr adventures with me, for the review and pictures.

Introduction

Trust me when I say that 'I know' it sounds crazy that I am best friends with a rooster and it certainly never started out as the end goal for either one of us but that's what happened. And like most friendships, it didn't happen overnight because actual true friendship requires a great deal of trust and that takes time to earn. So while we always, I assume, liked each other – he had to trust that I would not hurt any in his flock (a rooster's main priority) and I had to trust that he wasn't going to shred me with his spurs.

But gradually I began to see signs that I had earned his trust... He would stand in the rain at the front door and stare at it until I came out to pick him up or give him treats. He would run up to me when I got in the car, or on the tractor, mower or utility vehicle because he enjoyed going for rides. He would come and sit with me in the front yard and just watch the world go by. Of course, when all of that happened and I didn't get attacked my trust grew quickly.

At that point, Pokey Jr began coming into the house (when my wife wasn't around), sleeping on the back porch and we started going for coffee.

In addition... Well, it's all in the next few pages. Hope you enjoy getting to know a really cool rooster.

Prologue

This whole story begins when our family moved to the country to start a homestead. Well, it actually starts earlier and has its roots in a cross country lawn mower trip - but that is a much longer story. From that trip, we had desired a healthier way to live and a way to exist where we reduce our carbon footprint and start to slide off the grid. We would produce our own food, energy and find ways to recycle and repurpose everything.

So, back in 2008 we bought some land in east central Illinois and took the plunge. We had the great fortune of buying our land about five minutes before the economy went in the tank and the bottom went out financially. That created a three-year delay in actually getting to the next part of the plan but we got there and built a little home. Slowly and yet, sometimes recklessly, we took step after step until we got our first chickens (Hanibelle, Wanda, Pork Chop and Pokey) in early 2015.

Documenting that real life change led to the launch of the television show Coop Dreams, a show about our journey into homesteading. Had this not played out on camera, and in a way I could re-watch and confirm what was happening, I might not believe it myself.

The Hatch

In the on-going debate over which came first, the chicken or the egg, there's a noticeable lack of support for the incubator–and that's a shame as it's where this story begins. This little incubator arrived before the eggs and the chickens, so clearly - it came first.

Out in the chicken yard there are six nesting boxes. But the hens always lay in the exact same one. So when it was time to collect eggs to incubate, they were pretty easy to find. Four eggs were carefully selected. Three of various shades of brown and one beautiful light blueish egg clearly from Pokey, as she was the only Easter Egger in the flock. Easter Eggers lay uniquely colored eggs and have cute puffy feathers around their cheeks. Since she was the favorite hen, this egg was handled with extra care.

When the eggs were placed in the incubator, they all seemed pretty normal. Outside of being different colors none were much larger, much smaller or better shaped than any of the others.

Incubating is always a fun time and the excitement felt by the family was over the top. But when the chicks hatched, the outcome wasn't what anyone expected. They were weird looking. They kept stumbling around the incubator and falling over fast asleep. The poor chicks barely got any rest, they fell over so suddenly the family thought they were sick and would tap on the incubator to nudge them back awake. These wet and sticky looking things didn't match any of the pictures of the really cute chicks seen in magazines.

What a difference a couple of hours can make. By then, they were dry, really fluffy and very cute. The relieved family moved them to a larger box with room to run, scratch, peck and fall over.

In this box, the chicks discovered a feeder and waterer for nourishment, and a brooder for heat. As they approached the brooder, they felt its warmth. And as newborn chicks, heat is a very, very good friend. The chicks soon found they could walk under the brooder when they were cold and instantly find warmth and comfort... just like under a mother hen. Every chick knows it's so much better to fall asleep in a warm space. All the chicks seemed healthy and happy. Each, as with any hatching, was special in its own unique way. They were all equally held, loved and cuddled by their family while growing up. This loving attention made them very comfortable and very, very well-adjusted socially. There was a rhythm of contentment about them and they were completely happy to simply be cute little chicks.

Throughout their chickhood, the family noticed the hatchlings inseparable bond. When one scratched and pecked, the rest raced over to join in. When one found treats, the others jumped in quickly to 'share.' It was that way through their first few weeks and was pretty awesome to witness.

The brooder became a constant whirlwind of exploration and activity, sprinkled between moments when every chick collapsed in a nap. But, outside of the sudden napping something was always going on. There was eating. Scratching and pecking. Drinking. Playing. And lots and LOTS of pooping.

Brooder life was good. There really was no danger to worry about. Basic needs like warmth, food and water were always satisfied, leaving the chicks free to play and learn. In those moments when there was more poop than clean flooring, the giant hands of the chicken keeper entered and cleaned up all of the 'soiled' bits of bedding.

The chicks loved this magical, comfortable time free of adult worries and concerns. The sense of safety they felt in the brooder, is often a rare feeling for a chicken. The full feeder, waterer and clean bedding were also rare for a chicken. But the biggest game changer was the constant doting, cuddling and attention they enjoyed as cute, fluffy chicks.

Like most good things, life in the brooder couldn't last forever. After many weeks of loving care and the same scenery, out they headed on a new adventure. Dramatic changes lay ahead as these chicks moved to the great outdoors. Here, in a larger area they experienced grass and bugs for the first time.

This new pen, located in a protected area just outside the chicken yard, allowed every adult chicken to become familiar with the chicks. Gazing through the hardware cloth, the adults were unable to physically interact but they gave the chicks a good once-over with their eyes.

The notable physical differences living outside were many. Temperatures fluctuated a lot more. The poop didn't seem to be cleaned up quite as often and the feeder and waterer were not filled as frequently.

But, perhaps the biggest change were those adult chicken eyes fixated on the chicks all day, every day. The pen, an important part of a long-range transition and integration plan, allowed all of the adult hens to spend much of their non-scratching hours admiring the chicks. The chicks would stare back, but there isn't much that can hold a chick's attention for too long and they soon returned to scratching and pecking practice.

It didn't take long for the chicks to fully feather. While still cute, they were not the same irresistible fluff balls that attracted virtually 24/7 attention. With their new feathers came fewer faces looking into the pen and fewer cuddling sessions with the family. The feeder sometimes dropped to half empty AND sometimes some dirt was kicked into the waterer and not immediately cleaned. This was both an interesting and uncomfortable reality for the chicks, but all in all, life was still really good for them.

Living close to the chicken yard did have the advantage of hearing adult chicken-talk and learning the sounds and language of the flock. The more they heard, the more they learned and understood. Since they heard many of the same things, day in and day out, some phrases they picked up quickly:

"I think I'll go broody this spring... I really should before I get too old."

"They're sooooo cute. If I had fingers, I'd pinch their cheeks."

"Dear me, did we poop that often when we were chicks, Betty?"

And of course the reply that had them all cackling...

"Uhm, Gertie, you still poop that often."

The chicks, as they do, became more independent and less needy with each passing day. Not only were there physical changes, personality changes also began to emerge. Before, they all did the same kind of things, hung out together in the same areas and followed each other's behavior.

But now, each of the chicks was beginning to show their uniqueness and personality. While they each had a different mother, there was only one rooster, Edward, and since he was a combination of breeds, these chicks were all barnyard mixes.

Lumpy, a beautiful mix of caramel and black feathers, became skittish, jumpy and nervous about everything. It's understandable, because when Lumpy was born, she had a big red lump near her bottom. And while the other chicks never seemed to notice, there were a lot of concerned sounding whispers from outside the brooder box. Though Lumpy could not understand a single word, the tone and finger-pointing let her know something wasn't quite right. Luckily, after a few days, the little lump fell off and all was good. However, the early trauma left Lumpy with a sense of constant worry and anxiety.

In an exhaustive search for names, Red's, very clever name was inspired by her reddish brown color. A bit of a tag-a-long, Red just kind of followed whoever seemed to be the most fun. It wasn't because she was indecisive or uncertain, Red was just a very even-tempered hen that never seemed to get too up or too down. She just was kinda relaxed about everything.

Stormy, on the other hand, was playful and seemed to always find a way to knock over the waterer or the feeder, creating some sort of chaos wherever she went. A living example of her name, she stormed into every moment of her life. Stormy was stunning, all white with little puffy cheeks.

But, the fourth chick was different, and everyone noticed. As he grew, he began to show himself as an independent and free-thinking leader - a true rooster. It wasn't anything specific that created this sense, he just glowed with energy and presence. When this little fella came around, everyone took notice. Few could help but recognize his unique coloring - he seemed to have every color of the rainbow represented in his feathers.

Hatched from an egg laid by Pokey, his leadership and confidence were of little surprise to the flock – and without hesitation, he was named Pokey Jr. Pokey, the matriarch and the heroic figure in the chicken yard, had long served as an inspiration to the other chickens due to tales of her incredible survival skills and her independent personality. Rumor had it that Pokey survived six months trapped between bales of hay in the barn. Eventually, so the fable goes, Pokey grew stubborn enough to just push the bales away in order to escape. Through the years, Pokey always tried to set the record straight and pull back the many embellishments, but the fable was often told when she wasn't around to correct it.

Rumors, as they often do, grew through the constant re-telling. Pokey's sister, cleverly named Sis, always jumped in and pushed the narrative.

"It was 5… Only 5 months… A lot of chickens say 6 but it was really only 5. I know that because I looked for her every day." Sis was often heard to say.

Regardless of the timing, and the actual details, there was enough truth in the legend that it created an aura around Pokey as a survivor – a hen that never quit and never gave up. This was a very important quality for a mother hen to have, especially when raising a young rooster trying to find his way.

Pokey knew raising Pokey Jr would require the support of all the hens, but one for certain – Sis. Sis LOVED Pokey and Pokey loved Sis right back. But Sis was different. She was a bit neurotic, her eyes never seemed to be looking in the same direction at the same time, and some of her feathers always seemed like they were upside down or sideways. No matter how long you looked, you could never quite figure out if there was a pattern and organization to those feathers, or if she just woke up and hadn't quite shaken herself together.

Each day, all the hens came to the edge of the chicken yard to see the chicks, then eventually returned to scratching or bathing. But Pokey and Sis did not. With Sis by her side, Pokey stayed at the edge of the chicken yard admiring all the chicks. But, day after day, her gaze fixated on Pokey Jr. She knew he was her boy. She knew at some point; he would be the next leader of the flock. The way he walked and the noises he made, reminded her of her younger self, but the biggest giveaway were the fluffy and puffy cheeks. No one in the chicken yard could match Pokey's amazing cheeks and full beard. Now, Pokey Jr proudly displayed this exact same set of adorable cheeks.

Pokey Jr's father, Edward, also fathered all the other chicks as he was the only rooster in the chicken yard. And while Edward did venture over to look at the chicks frequently, his main job of protecting the flock did not offer the opportunity to stop and stare as much as he wanted.

As the chicken yard's only rooster, Edward took great pride in his powers of protection. He was an interesting guy, and none of the hens had really figured him out though Pokey probably came the closest. Edward loved her and opened up to her.

Edward had been adopted and brought to the farm when he was two, contributing to his air of mystery. No one knew his backstory or upbringing which are important details when establishing a pecking order and trust around the chicken yard. In the end, whatever the hens didn't know about Edward's past they filled in with their own imagination and gossip, adding to his air of intrigue.

Edward took his rooster role very seriously. When he found food, he was selfless in tidbitting and ALWAYS ate last, keeping his head up and watching for danger so the others could enjoy their bugs without worry. In addition, he frequently attacked anyone and anything he felt was a threat to his flock, and that made him VERY well respected within the chicken yard.

Edward spent a good deal of time discreetly studying the chicks, looking for personalities and potential future threats to his own leadership. One chick really began to stand out to him, and that chick was Pokey Jr. With Pokey as his mother and Edward as his father, it was no surprise that he began to exhibit the grace and strength of both his parents.

When the humans came round to visit the chicks, Pokey Jr was rarely scooped up for cuddles and conversation – but that was his choice. Fiercely independent, Pokey Jr neither wanted or needed any human contact. Instead, he focused his love and attention on his father. For hours Pokey Jr followed Edward, watching how he effortlessly, but sternly, ruled the chicken yard. Not every chicken agreed with Edward, but they all respected him and knew him to be a fair and just rooster.

Days and weeks passed, and Pokey Jr grew up in the comfortable position of a chick who is the son of the most respected hen and the most respected rooster in the chicken yard. Every other chicken in the flock knew who Pokey Jr was and knew who his parents were. To him, it was just a fact and he felt neither arrogant or entitled by his birthright. As Pokey Jr matured, he naturally began to climb in the pecking order. The change was very natural and not forced, so it caused no tension with any of the other chickens. In addition to showing good leadership, Pokey Jr had a great sense of humor, was friendly and related well to everyone. All these qualities created a unique set of relationships where the older chickens looked out for him but also respected him. His hatchmates idolized him and as more chicks came out of the brooder and joined the flock they, of course, thought Pokey Jr was the greatest thing ever.

Life was good for Pokey Jr but that's pretty common for chickens that are loved, respected and feel very, very important.

The Teens

Once the chicks reached their teens and could almost take care of themselves, their humans moved them into the main chicken yard. The transition went without incident.

Edward did an amazing job of keeping everything and everyone safe in the big yard. This eliminated much of the normal stress and anxiety that a chicken typically feels.

Pokey Jr, while mature for his age, bounced back and forth between playing with his chick pals, hanging out with mom and Sis and following his father around to study how one runs a chicken yard.

Luckily, he skipped that awkward period usually experienced by roosters and moved from chick and into adolescence pretty seamlessly. This was partly due to who he was inside and partly due to who he was to others. Anytime Edward belted out a loud crow, Pokey Jr tried to follow, but the crows were not as strong or impressive. Some of the hens smiled and some chuckled as it was pretty cute to watch the lil rooster who loved and respected his father so much.

Occasionally, when a hen ventured farther away from the flock than Edward liked, he rounded them up and headed them back to safety. During the process, Edward administered some very stern and scolding squawks to the wandering hens. Often, Pokey Jr would add in a few scolding squawks of his own after Edward finished. It was funny to watch the teenage rooster get so serious and the hens did a marvelous job of playing along. They knew that this practice was an important part of the continued development and protection of the flock.

These indirect learning opportunities were very valuable in helping Pokey Jr develop and polish his roostering skills. But, they could not serve as the only way to learn and so Edward would occasionally pull Pokey Jr aside to discuss 'important' rooster stuff.

"*PJ... Come here.*" Edward said softly so as not to alarm the other chickens. "*Come watch the hens eat.*"

Pokey Jr did as asked, but wasn't sure what they were doing or why.

"*Do you see that?*" Edward asked.

Pokey Jr didn't know what he should be looking at, or looking for, and didn't want to embarrass himself so he just softly nodded. After a few more seconds of not knowing, he gathered up all his courage and asked.

"*Dad, I'm not sure what I'm supposed to be seeing.*"

"*Look at the hens eat and tell me what you notice.*" Edward added not willing to give him the answer.

"*Some scratching... Some pecking....*" Pokey Jr said hesitantly and with no confidence that he was seeing the right thing.

Edward was excited in his reply. "*Right, right... What you don't see are any of the hens scanning the tree line, looking for hawks or mentally registering where there's cover.*"

Pokey Jr nodded but wasn't sure why.

"*None of them are ready if a predator were to strike. No one in that group is locked in on anything big picture.*" Edward continued as Pokey Jr looked over the hens again.

"*That's our job, that's our purpose... It is up to us to be locked in and focused on predators and security.*"

And now Pokey Jr understood, not just the words but the passion in his father's voice. Every time the two of them spoke, he understood a bit better what it means to be a rooster. And his chest swelled with pride and purpose.

Despite having taken big steps in his growth, Pokey Jr was still just a teenage rooster. Teenagers can only concentrate on adult things in limited doses. As soon as the dust settled on 'rooster school', Pokey Jr ran back to chase bugs with Stormy.

JR Rooster Police

filled with new knowledge on roostering, but also filled with the impatience of a teenager, Pokey Jr raced over to Pokey and Sis to see if they would notice how much he had grown as a rooster.

Back and forth he walked, before them, with his tail feathers held very high. He didn't often walk this way, but Pokey Jr felt very proud and wanted his mom to also notice.

Somehow, moms just know these things. When Pokey saw him strut, she smiled. She had seen this before in other young roosters, and it was a bit funny for her to see it in her little boy.

But, nothing can wreck a rooster faster than losing confidence. So before Pokey Jr could see his mom smiling she looked away and turned towards Edward. Edward simply nodded, recognizing what was going on and Pokey's work on protecting her growing boy's confidence.

Neurotic Sis, however, chimed right in when she saw the jaunty new angle of Pokey Jr's tail feathers. Never quite sure what was going on, Sis had never been a mother hen, and rarely said anything appropriate or at the correct time...

"Pokey Jr, what's with the tail feathers? Is your vent not feeling right?"

Sis knew better than any other chicken the difficulty of walking correctly when poop 'debris' gets stuck in your vent feathers.

Coming from anyone else this might have been a tragic hit to Pokey Jr's ego, but it was just Sis. Everyone knew Sis to be a bit different and socially awkward. So Pokey Jr let the comment go, but his tail feathers did droop a bit.

Pokey quickly shot Sis a look familiar to all.

"What? There might be something clogged up in his vent that's causing him to look so ridiculous." Sis responded.

"Hey sweetie go hang out with the girls, I hear there are some treats coming." Said Pokey while shaking her head at Sis. But, by this time, Sis had forgotten everything she had seen and was following a trail of slime hoping to find a delicious slug on the other end.

An unhappy Edward observed the sister's exchange, hoping his lessons from this morning would not be lost due to Sis. Edward turned towards her, but as he did, Pokey raised a wing slightly and shook her head in a signal to leave it alone. She knew both Sis and Edward well. She understood that strong, proud Edward, confronting Sis and her random memory would not lead to a productive conversation. Pokey also knew her son and understood this would not be a lasting set back. That is, unless it blew up into a bigger deal in the chicken yard. And so Edward, knowing Pokey was usually right in these moments, let it go and went back to his job as lead rooster.

Pokey Jr raced over to the girls with his tail feathers, a bit droopy now, but still held higher than normal. Busy scratching and pecking and excited over the rumors of treats coming soon, none really commented on the subtle change in Pokey Jr. Despite Sis's comments, and the girls lack of reaction, Pokey Jr was still very excited to be a more knowledgeable and stronger rooster.

With a sense of pride, he went right to work practicing his new found skills. He stood taller and scanned for predators as he had seen Edward do earlier in the morning. Immediately, his attention was rewarded as he spied their chicken keeper on the way with treats. He excitedly let out a little squeaky squawk to inform his girls first, and the entire chicken yard second, of the coming treats. It surely wasn't the best 'treat alert' any chicken had ever heard, but it was first, and so that was something to be very proud of.

Once he realized that he had been first to scream 'treats,' Pokey Jr beamed with pride and looked for both Pokey and Edward to see if they had noticed. When he found both and saw them each nod their approval his tail feathers shot back up. A big, BIG moment for a young rooster.

When the treats finally arrive, the chickens were thrilled to see their favorite – cooked spaghetti. And as usual, some of the hens grabbed a noodle and ran, while others jumped in to chase. Lumpy snatched a noodle immediately, concerned that if she didn't pounce on one of the first ones there may not be any left for her. True to their personalities, Stormy opted to chase her and Red followed along just to see what all the fuss was about.

As a young rooster, once you're full of pride and developing your leadership skills, it is tough to turn that off. So, while Edward watched, Pokey Jr decided to try out his authority. Off he ran after his girls, stepping boldly between Lumpy and Stormy and stopping their chase. No one would get hurt on his watch. Pokey Jr knew that roughhousing, statistically, was one of the leading causes of getting hurt. Once he closed down the fun and games, he escorted Stormy and Red back to the pile of spaghetti and instructed them to get their own noodles.

While his back was turned, two older hens came over and grabbed Lumpy's noodle. So, while he was growing as a rooster, there was still much to learn. And some of that is the balance, displayed by Edward, of knowing which battles to fight and which to let go. One of a leader's toughest challenges arise from the fact that what is fair for some may not be fair for all.

New World Order

L ife was good, and on the fast track to being great. Edward had the chicken yard clicking like a well-oiled machine. Meanwhile, day by day Pokey Jr gradually moved further away from playful teenager and closer to mature adult rooster.

Red, Lumpy and Stormy took no notice of it, but they were his flock to protect.

And every day he did the little things needed to keep them safe, fed and happy. Both Edward and Pokey watched with great pride as their little boy rapidly developed into a strong young adult rooster.

While his mother and father noted every accomplishment and milestone, one thing that had changed was Pokey Jr no longer looked over to make sure that his parents were watching. It's all part of growing up, but that doesn't make it any easier on a parent when their babies need them, and their approval, a little bit less.

It's nothing personal. Just part of that big, and sometimes stupid, circle of life thing that parents and children experience. Pokey took it much harder than Edward did, or at least rather than Edward showed publicly.

So all in all, life was in a really solid place. But as sometimes happens, things suddenly went upside down in a hurry... and in a way that had never happened before. Edward, by his sheer strength and confidence, kept the chicken yard in line and predators at bay. No one ever dared to mess with him. Edward wasn't mean–he was just in charge.

But nature does what it does and hunger will often overrun fear. Edward's confidence and strength screamed to foxes that this flock was off limits. Eventually, the coming of spring and hungry babies in the dens overrode that red light, made it yellow and desperate foxes began lurking just on the outskirts of the chicken yard.

Not new to the protection game, Edward could feel 'it' and while he didn't know from which direction they were being watched, he did know there were eyes upon them. In times like these a roosters' adrenaline runs high, and their heads are up and on a swivel. Eating stops, to better keep an eye on the woods instead of being in the vulnerable position of pecking the ground. Edward knew danger was in the air, and called his flock closer to him as the feathers on the back of his neck rose and prickled.

It wasn't a matter of IF the foxes would attack–but rather WHEN they would attack. Edward knew it was coming and kept himself ready. Though his mindset changed, he made sure his body language remained exactly the same. In looking at him none of his flock felt any more stressed than usual. They completely trusted Edward with their security. Everyone knew predators existed, had heard the horror stories and were always cautioned to be on guard. But, the danger never truly felt real for anyone in the flock.

Pokey Jr hadn't lived through a predator attack, but he was genetically wired to know it was a dangerous possibility. So when the others scratched and pecked and while Edward stood watch, Pokey Jr bounced between two very different levels of responsibility.

And while Pokey Jr had never seen a predator, and wasn't 100% sure exactly what one looked like, he was a rooster and roosters have a way. So, even as this day seemed very similar to other days, the feathers on the back of his neck were a bit tingly - a new feeling for him. He wasn't quite aware of 'what' was happening but; he did know that 'something' was happening. Casually, he found himself drawing nearer to Edward, eating less and watching his dad more. That was little help, though, as Edward always looked like Edward.

Pokey Jr turned for a second, no reason other than a roosters' instinct. In that moment, life within the flock changed forever. Sis, wandering dreamily on the edge of the flock did not notice how far she had strayed from the safety of the group and Edward. Seeing the opportunity, a fox darted from the woods and made a mad dash at Sis.

21

Out of the corner of his eye, Edward picked up the blur of movement, and within a second had raced over, and with spurs blaring, threw himself between Sis and the fox. In the same moment, he signaled to the rest of the flock the 'rooster call' to take cover.

The hens did what the hens do, running to safety as Edward fought the fox to provide them the time to get away. Pokey Jr, frozen with his brain and instincts in two worlds, didn't flee and didn't move. Instead, he watched Edward work the fox. With feathers flying everywhere, it was difficult to tell who was winning but in the end, the desperation and hunger of the fox beat the desperation and duty of the rooster. Edward fought valiantly but fell to the fox. His quiet, limp body was quickly carried off by the predator.

Pokey Jr stood frozen in shock. His instinct as a young chicken was to run to the flock and hide. His instinct as a young rooster was to move to the flock to gather and protect them. His instinct as a son was to break down and cry at the loss of his father.

In the end, the rooster instinct kicked in and he chased down and gathered up the flock to move them all to safety. What he had just witnessed was still raw and surreal, and very hard to get his head around. When Pokey Jr got to the flock, the hens were all filled with sadness and fear. Except Sis who seemed unsure of what had just happened. The rest were devastated to have lost a vital member of the flock and were in fear from the fact that their protector was gone.

As the hens looked around in despair and confusion, Pokey Jr was amazed at what was happening within him.

Somehow, he knew - he just knew what to do - how to keep them close, how to move them as a group to safety and how to find them food. This knowledge amazed and surprised him –and caught a few of the others by surprise, as well.

Pokey was a mess; devastated to have lost her love. While the others returned to their chicken routines of scratching and pecking; Pokey could not. The fox had taken a piece of her, too. Sis, who normally doesn't notice things, noticed Pokey's sadness.

"Hey Poke – what's up? You look sad."

Pokey looked at her, actually shot her a look. After all, Sis drifting away from the flock enticed the fox to attack and meant Edward had to jump in. Pokey looked into Sis's eyes, and wanted to unload on her. But, again, held it in.

No one knew Sis like Pokey did and in many ways Pokey looked out for her sister more like another mom. She knew that Sis was a kind hen and never meant any other chicken any harm. It was tough to get mad at her, even in moments like this, because Sis rarely knew what was going on or her role in it. In fact, it wasn't clear if she knew Edward was gone or if Edward ever existed in the first place. There was no malice in it, it was just who Sis was, but she also was a hen with a giant heart. Pokey knew that if she unloaded on Sis and let her know that she had caused this current trauma to the flock, Sis would never be able to recover emotionally.

So she did what a good protective big sister does sometimes. She held her tongue.

"Nothing's up Sis, I'm good," Pokey replied.

"What do you mean?" Sis answered.

"You asked what's up."

"I did?" Sis looked confused.

"Yes, never mind." Pokey ended the conversation as she had done a hundred times before, and Sis returned to looking for bugs.

Pokey Jr gathered the flock near the coop under a massive pine. He could hear them reflect on Edward, the way Edward had run the flock and the heroic way he protected them in the end. Despite the tragedy of the day, Pokey Jr felt very, very proud when he overheard the comments.

Ready or not, Pokey Jr was now in charge. He knew it, and the flock knew it, too. Everything was different. His playful urges disappeared overnight as every moment was spent searching for food, or checking out the flock's location and of course, the constant search for predators.

While all members gratefully deferred to his leadership, one little chick stayed glued to Pokey Jr's hip. It was Patch. Like Pokey Jr with Edward, Patch seemed drawn to his presence and fascinated by how Pokey Jr did things. He knew that this lil Patch was likely a rooster. As the circle spins, life provided Pokey Jr as Patch's teacher. And in the end, Pokey Jr would prepare Patch for the day when he relinquished the flock to him.

New Sheriff in Town

*e*dward willingly and bravely gave his life to save his flock and in doing so the flock became Pokey Jr's. And while Pokey Jr was different from his father, much of his leadership was learned in two ways: watching Edward, and the genetics of a rooster. These made him very similar to his dad and that made it an easy transition for the flock as there weren't many noticeable changes.

Immediately after the fox attack, Pokey Jr kept the flock tighter and closer together as it was easier for him to watch and gain confidence as their leader. No doubt, since the fox had been rewarded by hunting in the chicken yard, it seemed likely to return looking for another meal. Thinking ahead, Pokey Jr moved the flock as far from the spot of the attack as he could.

As days built on days, Pokey Jr became more comfortable with his role as head of the chicken yard. He found he understood the patterns, movements and individuals in his flock. He was a bit torn that his initial flock of Lumpy, Red and Stormy now had to share his attention and protection with the other chickens. While he felt awkward about it, his old flock moved on easily. It is what chickens need to do.

Pokey Jr also began to pick up predator activity more easily and discovered he could stay a step or two ahead of any dangerous moments. With that comfort, and the passage of time since Edward's loss, the flock was able to relax a notch or two and the chickens began to spread out a little more every day.

Pokey quietly stayed close by her son. While she knew he was ready for this role, she was still his mom and couldn't bear the thought of losing both Edward and Pokey Jr, even though that is the way that life in the chicken yard goes. And, she felt another set of eyes around him may be of great importance. Pokey gave up her feeding time to scan the yard and the sky for predators, but didn't mind as she had little appetite these days. Before long, she began to look thin and a bit sickly; even more so when she was standing next to Sis who never missed a meal.

Assuming leadership of the chicken yard comes with a lot of responsibilities and Pokey Jr loved them all. There was the rewarding role of treat finder and gathering the flock when he located food. As their lookout, he had to be aware of everything happening on the outskirts of the flock. Like most roosters, his favorite role was 'breeder' – the job of keeping the flock growing through the addition of new chicks. But, Pokey Jr saw training and teaching, this next generation, as his most critical role.

Edward, had been known as a great teacher and Pokey Jr felt driven to be a great role model cut from that same stone.

Patch, also a son of Edward and Pokey Jr's half-brother, continued to follow him everywhere, just as Pokey Jr once did with their father. And for the most part it was pretty cute. But, now and then Pokey Jr's frustration bubbled up as Patch was always under his feet. In those moments, Pokey Jr could clearly understand those times when his father's patience appeared short for no reason.

But Pokey Jr understood, all too well, how fragile life is and how quickly it can change. It was truly important to ensure that Patch grew to be a strong leader that can keep the flock happy and healthy when the day came that Pokey Jr was ready to turn it over to him.

From experience Pokey Jr knew that brave head roosters do not often run a flock for very long. The dangers they face, and the weight they carry, take a toll and shorten their lives. Regardless, these were good times. Pokey Jr was enjoying every day as the flock was happy and healthy, and he had kept them free from any form of predator attack for nearly a year. Finally, his confidence had grown to match the size of his job and he was comfortable in the position.

The tremendous responsibilities assumed by a lead rooster create a highly elevated stress level. But like his father, Pokey Jr maintained a very calm exterior. This allowed the flock to feel safe and comfortable and it also made them quite attentive when he used a more urgent and serious tone.

Pokey Jr's life, outside of the tragic loss of his father, had always felt 'important' but now as the lead rooster every action, every day and every moment were critically relevant.

Patch

atch was an interesting lil chick – a barnyard mix
larger than Pokey Jr and with a darker shade of
caramel coloring. Everybody thought Patch was a
rooster because of the way he carried himself. The fact that
Patch followed and adored Pokey Jr made it all the more clear.
Patch's hero worship reminded Pokey Jr of the way he had
viewed their father Edward.

Young Patch was very different from a young Pokey Jr,
however. As a chick, everyone loved Pokey Jr. Not because

he was next in line, but because he was a funny, kind and strong-willed chick that treated everyone well.

Patch, on the other hand, was different. While the others didn't find him very funny, Patch was kind and rarely crossed lines with anyone. So, while there was nothing specific that anyone could put their beak on. Patch was not well liked. He never did anything wrong, never treated anyone badly and never was a mean guy. But, he seemed to rub everyone the wrong way. Because all the chickens were well-mannered, no one ever said anything negative to him. They just passive-aggressively avoided him.

The chicken yard contained four coops and the chickens were allowed to spread out and roost wherever they chose. Mostly the chickens spread out evenly, more concerned with space than a particular coop mate. However, when Patch chose a coop, one by one the others left and moved to a different coop. Pretty soon Patch was sleeping by himself every night. For a while, he tried switching coops with the idea that there must be a draft or something. But, after a few weeks of switching coops every night and still waking up alone, Patch realized that the other chickens just didn't like him. While this made him sad, it was what it was. Rather than fight it and draw more attention to it, Patch accepted the situation and realized he would sleep alone every night.

As the leader of the chicken yard Pokey Jr, of course, stepped in and tried to fix this so Patch would not sleep alone. But, after he had all of the hens tucked in the coops for the night Pokey Jr's job was done and he didn't take note of where Patch was sleeping.

While Patch was sad that none of the hens accepted him, he was strong willed and just started hanging out with the goats. They were fairly new to the chicken yard, still trying to figure everything out, and kind of a bit crazy. The goats were fine with Patch hanging out with them and seemed to enjoy his company.

In the mornings, during feeding time, Patch ate with the goats, even eating their goat feed. It wasn't because he preferred goat feed to chicken feed, it was that they let him join in as an equal and did not leave when he showed up. A far cry from when he ate with the chickens as they would all scatter quickly.

At night, after a bit, Patch would sleep with the goats in their hut. While he preferred to roost in a coop, the goats were fine with him sleeping in their hut and made him feel welcome.

Though Patch clearly fell on the outside of the flock social structure, he was still wired to be a rooster. During the day, Patch would either follow Pokey Jr – or watch him from afar. Pokey Jr continued to mentor Patch and prepare him to lead the flock one day. And while Pokey Jr felt Patch was 'not normal', he still loved him and knew he was the future and needed to be well trained. Pokey Jr noted the differences and oddities but had bigger issues to worry about.

The long and cold winter arrived and decided to stay awhile. When spring finally hit, hungry foxes, raccoons and coyotes were evident everywhere. Pokey Jr's radar worked overtime as he was constantly spotting predator activity and moving the flock to safety. But, predators are sneaky and figure out how to work around preventative measures rather quickly. Soon, weekly attacks became the rule rather than the exception. While Pokey Jr was able to stop many, some still broke through.

This was devastating to the flock and to Pokey Jr, in particular. A rooster's main job is flock protection. When predator losses occur week after week, a rooster's confidence is always impacted. While the flock still believed in Pokey Jr, they were very concerned about their safety and well-being. Nobody said anything, but Pokey Jr felt it and the pressure and stress weighed heavily on him.

The toughest hit came when a predator took Red. Red was not only part of the flock, she had been part of HIS initial flock. Her loss was almost too much to bear.

That spring, predators were out at a level no one had ever seen. Also, the flock was now too big for one rooster to manage and protect successfully. Patch was, perhaps, not yet old enough to carve out his own hens to protect. And there was still the issue that he was not fully accepted by the flock.

While the responsibility of being the lead rooster gave great meaning and importance to Pokey Jr's days, it also came with a great deal of pressure, self-doubt and the scrutiny of the other chickens. Pokey Jr didn't let it show but he was losing confidence in himself as a leader. He was beginning to doubt that he was able to fulfill his purpose and role as the lead rooster.

None of the chickens really picked up on Pokey Jr's issues as there were many other things to focus on. Where to bathe today? Where do I sit in the pecking order? And, what is the best sleeping stick for me? But Patch noticed. Maybe it was because he was out of the main chicken loop. Maybe it was because he was a rooster and wired to see these things. Either way, Patch recognized the change in Pokey Jr.

Change Ain't Easy

Pokey Jr was too consumed with the job of keeping the dangerous outside world away, to clearly see much of anything going on inside the flock. But Patch, as next in command, focused only on the flock dynamics inside the chicken yard. Patch's observations led his internal monitor toward a growing lack of confidence in Pokey Jr's leadership.

Early one day, just after the morning feeding, instinct took over. Patch decided it was his time to lead, and made a sudden play to take over the flock. He charged at Pokey Jr, who was unprepared for an attack from the inside. Soon, both were crouched down with their hackle feathers flared out and eyes locked, circling one another over and over again. The entire chicken yard stopped, stared and held their breath. Patch struck first, flapping his wings as he threw his spurs and caught Pokey Jr's comb and immediately drew blood.

A transition in pecking order or flock leadership is never easy and always comes with some pain. During Pokey Jr's rise to power, there was the pain of the emotional loss of his father, Edward.

When it was Patch's time to take over, it was the physical pain of Patch's strength that Pokey Jr had to confront. Patch younger, stronger and far more confident seemed to hold the advantage. Pokey Jr had aged a lot with all of the stress of being in charge. And with his confidence down, he was unable to put up the strength of resistance this challenge would require.

Pokey was torn as she watched this battle. Of course, she was saddened that her son's leadership was being questioned and challenged. But – and perhaps this is how any mother feels when a son comes home from war - if Patch became the lead rooster, Pokey Jr would no longer be the flock's first responder. No longer would he be on duty 24 hours a day and no longer would he be the one to face the dangers on future predator attacks. So, in Pokey's mind there was a sliver of a silver lining.

The rational decision, when you are older and less confident, is to back away from a fight with a younger and stronger foe. But two things were at play: 1) Pokey Jr was wired, as all roosters are, to never back down. And 2) In order to make sure Patch was truly ready to lead and protect the flock he needed to fight for the position and be strong enough to take it. This would prove to the flock, and himself, that he was ready to actually do the job. So the reality was that the irrational decision was the right one for the betterment of the flock. And that was the decision that Pokey Jr chose.

When it was over, Patch had escaped without a single scratch. But, Pokey Jr was bleeding from so many injuries it was hard to see them all. After performing his final duty for the flock – ensuring that Patch was indeed ready to take over - Pokey Jr staggered away, making sure everyone saw, and knew, that Patch was now in charge.

The Newer Sheriff in Town

W hen the lead rooster is lost to a predator, the transition to the next leader is somewhat a clear and easy path. But when the next-in-line initiates a challenge and just takes the title, the transition becomes much more clouded and difficult. The flock often takes sides, with some in favor of the change, and others wishing things would remain the same. When it is a hostile takeover, and the old leader is still in the flock, it creates constant tension.

While Pokey Jr had accepted the role of second rooster, Patch always felt he was being evaluated and compared to the great leader that Pokey Jr had been.

Patch was not as naturally confident as Pokey Jr, a likely outcome of the years of rejection he faced as a teenager. That ding in confidence created a problem that only grew worse with Pokey Jr still in the chicken yard. His presence was a constant reminder to Patch that he would likely never measure up to Pokey Jr's status in the minds of any of the hens.

Initially, it was just a bother that Patch lived with. But as time moved on, the nagging self-doubt became both a distraction and an annoyance. Despite his poor start as a chick, Patch actually began to become a really solid and good leader of the flock. He still wasn't 'normal' by chicken standards, but after multiple defensive successes against predators, and no hens lost, the flock developed great confidence in Patch. While, he still felt the flock didn't like him personally, he knew they all felt safe with him in charge and took great comfort in that.

Over time, Patch gained confidence and grew into the role of leader. But Pokey Jr's presence continued to bother him. Eventually, and likely on a bad day, Patch decided that for him to fully lead the flock, Pokey Jr must leave and he went to 'confront' him.

Pokey Jr had sensed Patch's discomfort so he chose to stay in the far corner of the chicken yard, leaving only to eat or drink. That, however, was not enough for Patch who wanted Pokey Jr gone and out of sight. This desire moved Patch to violently attack and with no room for escape, Pokey Jr took another bloody beating with little resistance.

Regardless of his position in the pecking order, the hens still cared for Pokey Jr. This beating was difficult for the flock to watch, and absolutely devastating for Pokey.

It wasn't lost on Pokey Jr that Patch wanted him gone, but that meant a lonely existence living outside the fence. Living in the dangerous zone beyond the fence perimeter also might mean a very short time left on the planet. So, while his leaving was best for Patch, perhaps best for the flock, it wasn't a great situation for Pokey Jr. After weighing all options, self-preservation kicked in and Pokey Jr decided to stay and tough it out.

Day after day, Patch continued to pound home the point that Pokey Jr wasn't welcome in his chicken yard. Pokey Jr would take a beating in the morning and stay in the corner the remainder of the day. Patch was a kind and fair rooster and struggled to continue his attacks; but roosters are wired to remove obstacles that prevent them from being the best leader they could be. Pokey Jr's presence was an obstacle for Patch.

The impact of the daily conflict was massive and rippled through the entire flock. For Patch, the frustration he felt that Pokey Jr refused to leave, created greater strength in his attacks.

For Pokey Jr, it was as bad as it could ever get for a rooster. Physically he took a pounding every day. The strain of the beatings was wearing on him. His pride and confidence both fell to the lowest possible point. He had moved from the highest place of leadership to cowering in the corner. That by itself was demeaning. But the fact it happened in front of his flock and his friends was devastating.

The other chickens, who in reality, still loved and respected Pokey Jr, felt badly for him. They simply couldn't stand the emotional pain of seeing the sad state he was in. To avoid the depressing sight, they began to hunt and peck and gossip on the other side of the chicken yard, out of sight of poor Pokey Jr. As a result, the days seemed long and pointless to him, with very, very little social interaction.

Lumpy and Stormy were exceptions and provided a bright spot in the day. Each morning, they stopped by to say hello and share a bit of news. But the visits created a strain on them all, and gradually the two came less and less – until finally they just stopped coming.

Sis would occasionally walk by and say hello, but she had no idea what was going on. That was a relief, as she was the only hen unchanged in how she treated him.

Pokey, on the other hand, was always nearby. She brought treats, hung out and tried to be the best mother and friend she could be. But her faithful attention made life even tougher for Pokey Jr. It was terribly embarrassing, as an adult rooster, to have your mother come to comfort and tend to you. While he appreciated what she was doing, each visit became more uncomfortable than the last. Pokey Jr wanted out. This was NOT the way he wanted to be seen or remembered.

The situation did make his appreciation for Edward that much greater. Edward's generous and gracious departure reflected the honorable way for a rooster to leave the flock and cement his lasting legacy. Pokey Jr's legacy by comparison, was one that no rooster would choose.

After a few more weeks of this, Pokey Jr could take no more. The risks of life beyond the fence were more appealing than the continued humiliation and conflict. In his mind, this would allow Patch to fully lead, would eliminate distractions for the flock and, of course, would stop the daily beatings at the spurs of the younger and stronger Patch.

With the decision made, Pokey Jr hopped the fence and began the next chapter of his life. He waited until dusk to try to eliminate anyone attempting to change his mind. Outside the chicken yard was an uncomfortable place. There was no fence for protection. No coop for shelter. No sleeping stick for roosting. No feeders or waterers. And no companionship.

But inside the fence, the chicken yard was back to a peaceful and tranquil place with only one rooster and an easy-to-understand hierarchy. Pokey Jr knew his decision had been the right one.

With Pokey Jr gone, Patch's confidence grew. And with no other rooster to think about, the flock locked in on him as their true leader. As their belief in his leadership grew, so did Patch's level of skill and diplomacy. Feuds were handled quickly and, by everyone's account, fairly. Pecking orders stayed consistent and the overall health and well-being of the flock flourished.

Predator sightings occurred frequently, but Patch was a big boy and was quick and relentless when he locked in. Additionally, he learned to read the predators. He grew to know their scents and sounds and to anticipate their movements and patterns. Able, at last, to direct all his attention to the local predators; he remained one step ahead.

While the flock still didn't like Patch much, they did learn they could trust him, which is actually a better thing to have as a leader.

Pokey had no ill feelings towards Patch, as she understood how important a positive flock dynamic is, and how it develops. But she did miss her boy and would often stand at the edge of the yard trying to get a glimpse of Pokey Jr. Even a quick sighting from a distance provided her a bit of peace of mind.

As the lead rooster, the flock began to accept Patch a bit more each day. When he went into a coop at night, it did not immediately empty as before, and those in his coop actually felt safer. This was his first experience with hens who chose to stay with him; he was both surprised and proud of the fact that he had earned the trust of the flock.

Life in the chicken yard was the best and safest it had ever been. The older hens not only knew it, but made sure to gossip about it with the younger chickens. To be fair, Patch's big advantage was the new livestock fence installed by the chicken keeper. The fence provided an extra layer of protection that helped Patch stay a step ahead of predators.

Looking back, Edward, the most heroic of the lead roosters, had no fence separating his flock from danger. So of course, his predator loss was the highest. Fencing had not been installed until halfway through Pokey Jr's time as lead rooster. Patch had a security advantage that was, of course, lost in the re-telling of the legacies of these fine leaders.

Initially, as the days went on, Pokey Jr stayed somewhat close to the chicken yard. Once you are a lead rooster, and it is in your DNA, you never really disconnect. Pokey Jr still needed to make sure his flock was safe and secure, so he watched from afar. And while it was rewarding to see that everyone was doing well, he felt even more comfortable that Patch was actually a really, really good leader. This realization gave Pokey Jr comfort, even though it was also very difficult to acknowledge that the flock had moved on and was prospering under the leadership of another rooster.

After a few weeks had passed, and he was secure in the knowledge that Patch had everything under control, Pokey Jr moved far enough away that the flock would be out of his eyesight completely.

While a tough move for Pokey Jr, it was crushing for Pokey, who now only had the rare sighting of her boy as confirmation he was still alive.

It wasn't easy, but it was a move he had to make for his own sanity. Life outside the fence, and away from the flock, was tough as predators could get you from all sides. Additionally, it was lonely–terribly, terribly lonely, as there were no other chickens living outside the chicken yard.

There were cats, horses, dogs and people–so there was something to ease the boredom. But it was a lonely new chapter in his life.

There were a few perks, though. First, there was never a line at the feeder, and he was grateful to see that there were feeders now on the outside as well. With fewer chickens, it is less likely that someone will poop in the waterer. If poop was in a waterer, then it belonged to Pokey Jr and he was very careful to never poop in his own waterer.

Another advantage was that the door to the back porch was often left propped open. That allowed Pokey Jr easy access to shelter in the rain and an old comfortable green bucket to roost on every night.

There was also an endless supply of tasty, but highly addictive cat food on the back porch and while no one would argue that cat food is delicious, it clearly wasn't designed for the digestive systems of roosters.

Flying Solo

Life outside the chicken yard was a pretty balanced combination of exciting, frightening and lonely. One of the benefits, was that Pokey Jr could roam the entire farm. He was the only chicken on the property that had that ability, so he could explore areas no one else could reach. The drawback to that is, of course, he had zero protection and zero companionship. There was no fence and no other chickens to hang out with.

Another plus, though, was his ability to get food and water with no competition. When he was in the chicken yard, sometimes he ate when he wasn't hungry simply because there was no line at the feeder. Outside the chicken yard, he could eat and drink when hungry and thirsty and not simply when it was convenient. This should have helped a lot with his ability to manage his weight however, the boredom of being alone often led to some binge eating that had his weight ballooning up.

Sometimes Pokey Jr would go to the chicken yard and just stay outside the fence so he could see and talk with some hens. But that didn't sit well with Patch and he would often charge Pokey Jr through the fence. Occasionally, Pokey Jr was put back in the chicken yard to see if all would work out. But it never did. It was more for the convenience of managing the food and water in one chicken yard because, of course, managing two chicken yards was twice the work for the chicken keeper. So, every time he was put in the chicken yard, it ended in a bloody Pokey Jr jumping out to safety.

The ability to talk to, connect and hang out with the hens through the livestock fencing was painful. It served as a constant reminder that he was too weak and unaggressive to run the flock. But it was his only connection to other chickens and had an internal value he could not fully understand.

The humiliation of being attacked through the fence and having 'his' old hens look at him with embarrassment was too much to handle on a daily basis. So Pokey Jr made the choice to never visit the chicken yard again. It was a major decision and one he didn't take lightly.

The tradeoff is an elevated level of loneliness. In his new world, Pokey Jr was the only chicken left on the planet.

Life wasn't good. Pokey Jr soon found himself with a heavy addiction to cat food. It wasn't easy for him to digest as the nuggets were large and it wasn't made for the nutritional needs of a chicken. But it was convenient, tasted good and became a comfort food. In addition, his life began to drift to the edge. He took chances and lived in a manner that certainly wasn't one that would lead to making it to the later years of one's life.

He had no companionship, lived on the edge of fox attacks and raccoon sightings and seemed to flaunt his visibility. It was almost as if he had a death wish and was looking for an end to the pain of being the only chicken in his current world. This self-destructive way of living wasn't the desire of Pokey Jr but it was what his days had become.

Sometimes life would shake itself up and allow him the opportunity to find some value to his day. This was often through the 'infirmary', a separate coop for rehab, that was located behind the house on the farm. Any sick or injured chicken would be moved to this secluded home to recover.

While it was a needed element for a sick chicken to have the space and comfort to heal, it was also a welcome moment for Pokey Jr. He felt guilty that he loved whenever there was an injured chicken, as it meant he would have some level of companionship, but it went against the internal drive of a rooster.

With an injured chicken in the infirmary coop and run, Pokey Jr charged himself with security detail on the outside. He patrolled the exterior of the run as if his life depended on it and worked hard to make sure the injured or sick hen felt safe by his presence. This gave him a sense of purpose he had not experienced outside the chicken yard and he took it very, very seriously.

On one occasion it was his mother, Pokey, that was injured. She had hurt her leg. He was SO EXCITED to be able to help and comfort his mother through her recovery. As she healed, he patrolled 24/7 (or at least until he was put to bed) and made sure that she felt safe and secure during her time in the infirmary.

Once the chickens recovered and were strong and healthy, they were returned to the flock. But during their time of recovery, Pokey Jr was there constantly. Once they returned to the chicken yard, so did the joy Pokey Jr felt in helping to protect them.

That created additional difficult times. Pokey Jr had no support group as the horses were frightened by his movements. The dogs were crazy and hyper whenever he was around. And the cats, well the cats could care less about anyone but themselves.

With that difficulty came a deeper dive into the 'at risk' lifestyle Pokey Jr had adopted and he would often venture far from the house to an area where foxes were known to strike.

Anyone witnessing this would look at it as a sign of bravery and strength. But internally, and while he didn't admit it even to his own consciousness, it was a cry for help. Because in some ways, the immediate pain of being taken by a fox would be less than the long-running pain of living the rest of his days alone.

There were no easy answers. So every day he woke up and fought through the depression and fought through the loneliness to continue to live as a rooster; and hope that one day, he would once again, have a flock that he could manage and protect. But until that day arrives, he had to work his way through the crushing feeling that he had as a rooster with no purpose.

Something's Brewing

The winter was a rough one and Pokey Jr struggled. Days were short, it was dark longer and it was freezing out. He no longer had the warmth of a few hens to nestle between in the coop. People and animals stayed inside longer so he had fewer and fewer interactions with anything or anyone.

This brought on a level of loneliness and sadness that was suffocating.

He found himself roosting on his bucket 20 of the 24 hours in a day and had little physical movement. Pokey Jr hadn't fully given up on life, but he was close enough to see that landmark from where he roosted.

Daily he wondered. Why go on? What's the point? He felt he meant nothing to anyone. If he wasn't around, who would care, or for that matter, even notice. It was not a good place to be and it found him grumpy and sleeping his days away. The Meow Mix hangover was a daily pain he had to deal with. It was the result of numbing his thoughts and feelings away and he felt it a fair trade.

As the snow began to melt and the days grew longer, the additional sunlight brought some lighter moments. But nothing really changed and happiness for Pokey Jr had started to be something he couldn't really remember ever experiencing. He began to attack people that came around the back porch. Sometimes it felt as if he were protecting his territory and sometimes it felt as if he were hoping they'd retaliate.

One Wednesday morning was different, even though it started the same as the last 52 Wednesday mornings, it was different. Like many days, when he heard the garage door open, he went around and into the garage to look around. Not because the garage was a cool, fun or a magical place, it was actually a mess with junk all over the place and not a really engaging place to be.

But in coming around from the backyard and in walking into the garage, it usually killed a minute of the day that would otherwise be spent alone and on the back porch. With

1,440 minutes to kill each day every minute he could put in the rear view mirror mattered. Even though each trip to the garage was equally uneventful, he took advantage of every one. But this one was surprisingly different. He might get two minutes out of it, because as he entered, he heard a different sound.

It was a faint sound, but a new sound to the garage. And that, for a rooster living as Pokey Jr did, was worth exploring. Following where the sound came from, he saw some flashy colors on a shelf that were not there on any of the other days.

He'd heard about incubators, and had seen pictures, but this was the first one he had seen in person. It was kind of an exciting find for him. Everyone loves chicks and is excited about them hatching and Pokey Jr was no different, as roosters are wired to be excited about this too.

Life had a different rhythm now. Sunlight was more abundant. Days felt warmer. And there were chicks coming! Now whenever he heard the garage door open, he raced around to see the incubator and to see if he could hear any of the sweet sounds of cracking eggshells that comes with pipping.

Pokey Jr was great at keeping track of days and he knew that eggs take twenty-one days to hatch. But what he didn't know, was when the eggs were placed inside the incubator. He had first seen them a week ago, so if that was day one then he had two weeks to go. There were seven eggs in the incubator, and while he did not know the success rate of the machine, he did think that five was pretty likely from a broody hen and that was what he expected.

As days passed, he found himself happier and getting more and more excited about seeing the new chicks. But that wasn't anything new, as there isn't anyone on the planet that doesn't think baby chicks are awesome.

A few days later, he noticed the noise had stopped, as did the turning of the eggs. From his days in the chicken yard, he remembered that broody's stop turning their eggs three days away from hatching. This was exciting, especially for a lonely rooster that is desperately searching for some meaning in his life and he could hardly sleep.

He had heard that chicks can hear their moms through their shells. So, when he would sneak into the garage, he would crow. Not to deceive them, but to provide them some comfort with a chicken-related noise. For the first two days there was no response. But on day three, he heard chirping and could hardly contain his excitement. It was an immediate connection to the babies, and it made him feel like a rooster again.

The next morning, he began crowing at around 2 AM, as he wanted everyone in the house awake and the garage door to open. He wanted to watch the chicks hatch. It wasn't a conscious thought, but it did pass through his mind that he would be the first chicken they would see and there was a chance they would instantly bond with him.

He tried to force out the thoughts of being a rooster again and protecting this small little flock, as he wasn't sure he was strong enough to withstand another blow to his fragile ego. But he couldn't and found his mind wandering back to rooster-like thoughts.

When he heard the garage door open, he raced around the corner, hopped up on a ladder and watched the eggs move a little as the chicks began to pip. From the ladder, he had a really good view. But the people were pretty excited, too, and they kept getting in the way. Thankfully they had to work and eventually left him with a clear view of the eggs hatching.

After a number of hours, six of the seven eggs had hatched. Each looked wet, sticky and a bit sickly, but that turned to fluffiness within an hour or so. Pokey Jr was amazed at how completely uncoordinated they were, and at first he was convinced that they were all defective. But within a few hours, they began to show a little improvement in their coordination and movements.

This was all so incredibly exciting. Pokey Jr didn't want to leave the garage and the baby chicks he felt driven to protect, but he was eventually shooed out and the door was closed behind him.

He went around to the back porch and jumped up onto his bucket for the night. There was clearly a very different spring in his step. First, there were chicks around, and chicks make everything better. Second, he was the only chicken on the farm that knew there were chicks and it's always kinda cool to be the only one, or the first one to know anything. And third, all of his rooster instincts were reappearing and his protective nature was beginning to kick back in.

The Importance
of Roostering

In one's life, days blend with days and they become difficult to sometimes separate one from the other. This makes unique and important days really, really special. Being a rooster is no different, and Pokey Jr who typically begins crowing around 4 AM, was very excited today and adjusted his schedule to begin crowing at 3 AM.

There were six baby chicks hatched yesterday and that has completely changed the rhythm of the farm - certainly of Pokey Jr's day. Roosters are wired to care for and protect others. It's one of the cool things about being a rooster, because your life has such clear direction. And if you follow that direction, your life has such incredible meaning.

And that, actually, has been the big problem for Pokey Jr. When his father, Edward, was lost he wasn't ready to be the lead rooster. In all honesty, few are, and they learn as they go, which Pokey Jr did and did really well. He went from fun loving teenager to flock security overnight and had to grow up fast. Having watched his father, he had a good handle on how a proper rooster runs a chicken yard and the transition was pretty seamless for the flock. In fact, it went so well, the respect and love he felt from his flock was incredible and provided another layer of meaning to his days. Although he didn't make any of his rooster decisions for love and respect, it was a nice perk.

As the lead rooster, every day was filled with incredible challenges that he navigated well. And with each correct twist or turn, he gained more confidence and fulfillment of his purpose. This made it crushingly difficult when Patch decided it was his time to take the title and transition Pokey Jr to a directionless existence.

When he thought about it logically, and without emotion, Pokey Jr fully understood and supported all the decisions, as it truly was in the best interest of the long-term health of the flock and chicken yard. But, sometimes the right thing to do comes with a heavy price, and Pokey Jr was the one who had to pay that bill.

This all built up to where Pokey Jr is today and why he is so excited. There are six chicks in an incubator that have no mother hen or rooster nearby to look over them. He was still wired to be a rooster, and these little six chicks needed a protector.

Was it possible? Do roosters ever get second chances to be roosters?

He had no idea what the answers to these questions were but he was beyond excited to find out.

Hello Chicks

The next day, when Pokey Jr raced into the garage, he was super excited to see that the fluffy chicks had been moved to the brooder. Now, outside of the incubator, he could see and respond to them better and knew his connection to them was sure to grow deeper and stronger very quickly.

It was amazing how quickly Pokey Jr's rooster genetics kicked back in. He would patrol the outside of the brooder in a similar manner to what he once did when he was running the chicken yard. While the garage proved an easier environment to protect, he carried himself as if it was a war zone. Every noise would cause his head to stretch and he'd scan the garage for any predator or potential hazard for the chicks. His vision sharpened to their 'pre-eviction' levels, and he would take note of anything different and out of place from the day before.

It's not possible that Pokey Jr was the father to any of these chicks, but you'd never know it by watching him, or them. They instinctively responded to him as they would to the rooster that was their father. They followed him with their eyes. They understood when he made noises at feeding time. And they instinctively understood his distress calls and would huddle together in the corner when he asked. Sometimes it was for practice and flock training, and other times it was when the garage door would open unexpectedly. Either way the bond between rooster and chicks was fully engaged.

During the first days when the chicks were in the brooder, Pokey Jr would sometimes hide out in the garage and try to be locked in at night. When that wasn't allowed, he would anxiously return to the back porch, but he could hardly ever sleep on his bucket anymore. The nights on the back porch lasted forever, as he battled the internal thoughts of being a protective rooster, while not being within eyesight of the chicks he was called to protect.

As time went on, the chicken keepers noticed how protective Pokey Jr was. They thought that a wise and prudent move would be to allow him to move from the back porch to the garage. This would be a welcome move and relieved a lot of the stress a rooster has when he cannot see his flock.

He took great pride in the quick and healthy growth of the chicks, and their constant playing and sleeping routine. With every day, there were noticeable changes in their ability to survive out in the real world. That was a huge sense of pride for Pokey Jr as it was the sole goal of his current life.

Occasionally one of the chicks would get stuck somewhere, have pasty butt or be under the weather, but Pokey Jr would work through all of those moments. With each of these challenges overcome, he would be pulled deeper into his affection for the chicks and they to him.

A good rooster is always looking one step ahead and spots changes and irregularities before they fully develop. Pokey Jr was on point in this capacity. He knew that the next step from the brooder is a grow-out pen, a separate area that is most commonly built beside an existing chicken coop or inside the coops run, secure enough to prevent the older chickens from attacking or harming the younger chicks, but allowing them the opportunity to see them. He was concerned about the chicks being ready for the move, the weather changes, the grass, bugs and other parts of the outdoor world that contained bacteria and elements that could be a danger to them. While his main concern was their safety, he was filled with anxiety wondering if he would still be allowed to protect them.

If the grow-out pen was outside the house, he would be able to provide a security detail for them every day. That was his expectation. However, he couldn't help but think about when they were old enough to integrate with the adult chickens, and if that meant they would be ripped from his care and moved to live with Patch and his flock.

And while he trusted Patch, and knew he was a good rooster, he also knew that there was no way Patch could provide the same level of protection to these chicks that he could. His thoughts NEVER turned to how his life, and how a return to rooster irrelevance would impact him. Pokey Jr's sole focus remained squarely on his role as the protector of this micro-flock.

Growing Up

The ups and downs of life had taught Pokey Jr many, many things. One of those is how badly he needed these chicks. He didn't 'need,' them as his life would go on and he would survive without them. BUT, he 'needed' them in a way that made value of his moments. Oddly enough the chicks, at this time, didn't actually need Pokey Jr, as all their needs were cared for. They were internally wired to just figure out how to be chickens. BUT their lives were better with him watching over them, and they learned quicker with him as their guide.

And as life always does, it moved forward. And for these chicks, that meant moving to the grow-out pen outdoors. At first, it was a part-time thing and only during the day. The temperature would drop at night, and they were not yet fully feathered. While this was more chaotic than Pokey Jr wanted, it did ease him into overseeing security, as he could relax a bit at night and be fully recharged for the next day's challenges.

Moving was an exciting adjustment for the chicks, as EVERYTHING was new. They had never seen or felt grass before and grass really is an incredible thing, especially if you've never known it even existed.

Additionally, in the garage, the only insects they ever saw were flies, and those were both tough to catch and disgusting to eat. Out here there were ants, beetles, slugs, worms and a variety of other delicious bugs. A BIG part of being outside was dirt and the ability to enjoy sweet soothing dust baths. While not seeming to be an attractive thing, it is important for the cleanliness of birds and the prevention of mites and other pests. What was amazing to Pokey Jr was that the chicks just knew how to dust bathe and didn't need to be taught. The stretching of the wings, the flicking of the dirt and the scratching is all genetic.

The move outside was exciting for Pokey Jr as well, as roosters enjoy being outside far more than they enjoy being in garages and on back porches. The sun, the air and the endless supply of insects was important to their overall health. The only drawback to being outside is that the garage really had zero predators to be aware of, while outside there were foxes, raccoons, possums, owls, hawks and coyotes.

In addition to all of those external threats, there were some other elements on the farm that proved to need his attention. There were three dogs, and even though they were all non-aggressive, they were playful and fast. That was alarming to both Pokey Jr and the chicks.

There were also two cats. Even though cats and birds typically don't mix, these cats really took little notice of the chicks as a meal and would just come to hang out to watch them because chicks are incredibly watchable no matter what species you are. Even though they never attacked or were aggressive, Pokey Jr trusted only himself. He would always keep an eye on them, and when he felt uncomfortable, he would chase them off. The cats could easily protect themselves or worse but they respected Pokey Jr. When he said play time was over, they agreed and left.

Despite a covered top on the grow-out pen, that protected the chicks from aerial predators, Pokey Jr wanted to ensure that the chicks understood the warnings for hawks and owls. Although there was no way for the chicks to be taken in this manner, he would loudly give the aerial predator alert when one appeared, to give the chicks the experience of taking cover and finding protection. This way, when older, they'd be ready.

And so, while he loved being back outside, he did feel an elevated sense of anxiety. Which wasn't a bad thing as this balanced the elevated sense of purpose. Kind of the trade off in the circle of the life of roostering.

Prior to the chicks being born Pokey Jr struggled to sleep. The emptiness of not fulfilling your destiny is a haunting feeling and did keep him up at night. Oddly enough he was sleeping far less now as every noise, every shadow and every movement put him on full alert. But the crazy part is, that even though he is sleeping less, he felt far more rested than in the months prior to the chicks being born. Much of this he attributed to the fact that a life of meaning allows a different peace of mind that spills over into other areas of one's life.

The chicks really thrived outside and were learning new and important things every day. As an observer, Pokey Jr took great pride in this as he knew it was his destiny to get them ready for chicken life. As they got to be fully feathered they began the transition to full time outdoor chickens and would spend the night outside but still in the protective confines of the grow-out pen.

While it is the natural and next step in their development, it was also the natural and next step in Pokey Jr's anxiety level. Without the evening protection of the garage, the chicks were available to predators all day and all night.

All of this growth and development was exciting, and of course part of life, but it also moved everyone closer to the next progression in the life of a developing chicken. Integration into the main chicken yard.

While still off and in the future, Pokey Jr did have in the back of his mind a wondering of the how's, when's and what's of the next steps and what his role would be in that new world. While still very locked in with chick-centric thoughts, being a rooster again was very addictive and not something he was interested in giving up.

Next Step's a Good Step

The big day was upon them and there was a nervous excitement in the air. The chicks were fully feathered, and like all fully feathered chickens, they wanted the independence and freedom that comes outside the grow-out pen. The chicks had wanted and felt ready for this freedom for about a week already, but they were not in control of these kinds of decisions. They did feel that with Pokey Jr around nothing would happen. So, why couldn't they be with the big chickens?

Knowing what was coming, Pokey Jr not only did his job, but made sure everyone was witness to it. It was out of character for him, but he wanted to make sure, that when the decisions were made on these chicks, that he would have shown himself to be indispensable to their safety and wellbeing. In all honesty, he was pretty nervous about what would happen and if he'd be allowed to continue watching over them.

The chicks were ready, and every movement outside the grow-out pen felt like it was the magical time for them to head 'downtown'. They were walking a bit different today as they were practicing looking tough and strong so that when they went into the chicken yard, the other chickens would know that they belonged.

Although grass surrounded them, everyone could hear the steps approaching as the time for the big move was upon them. The lid was lifted, the chicken keeper picked up each chick and placed them in a transport coop. Even though he knew everything that was to happen today, the fact that someone was handling his chicks, had Pokey Jr on edge. His radar was up and he was clucking up a storm. As the chicks were carried towards the chicken yard, Pokey Jr followed with his head up high, making agitated noises making sure the chicks knew he was nearby.

As they neared the main yard, Patch was on point and began alerting his flock to the approaching traffic. He had no idea what was happening, but knew it looked different and squawked loudly. Pokey Jr heard Patch and recognized the anxious tone.

The closer they got to the chicken yard, the more elevated everyone's blood pressure became. For Patch, his protective instinct kicked in. For the chicks, it was the excitement of the move to becoming 'big' chickens. And for Pokey Jr, it was both the anxiety of moving back into the chicken yard and the excitement of returning to the routine of a normal rooster.

It's crazy how life sometimes changes in a split second. Sometimes you see it coming and sometimes you don't. This time - no one saw it coming. The chicks were carried past the gate and everyone's energy immediately changed. Something was up, and nobody knew what it was.

Patch got calmer. Pokey Jr got more anxious, and the chicks got more confused. Soon, all anxiety turned to hope, as just past the main gate was a smaller, fully enclosed and vacant chicken yard. Was it possible that this would be their new home? Could it be that this fully secure play area was their next habitat? When the chicks saw it, they were freaking out. This was massive, in comparison to their grow-out pen, and they couldn't even imagine how many bugs were in there.

Pokey Jr had the same spike in excitement. But, it soon dropped when he saw the fully enclosed run. With a covered run what is the need for a rooster? He tried to be brave and tried not to overthink it, but he was beginning to feel as if he would be left out.

When they arrived at the new chicken yard, the chicks were each placed in the run. They ran around and around and around in excitement as there were so many new and crazy things to see. There were play areas, perches, new waterers and new feeders, a really cool coop, rocks, dirt, everything a chick could want. They were so excited; they didn't give a second thought to the main chicken yard or where their protective rooster could be.

Pokey Jr, on the other hand, watched with both pride and concern as the chicks raced around the run like their feathers were on fire. Moments before the door closed, on the new chicken run, Pokey Jr was scooped up by the chicken keeper. He was held for a minute or two, at least in his mind, and then the world slowed down to an almost complete stop. His life flashed before his eyes and images of his loneliness raced through his mind. In an instant, and before he could even realize what was happening, he was gently placed in the run with the chicks and the door was closed behind him.

The relief Pokey Jr felt was incredible. His rooster instincts were immediately back in full force as he made sure his chicks didn't fall off the perches, that no one overate, and that the door was secured behind them.

Like a disciplined rooster, he patrolled the outer edges of the run to see if there were any soft spots that predators could exploit. Seeing none, his next task was a coop inspection. Was it sturdy and secure? Did it have proper ventilation? How many entrances and exits? Once it passed inspection, he was able to relax a little, enjoy the chick's excitement and savor the fact that his ability to 'be' a rooster had just been extended.

Soon life moved into what the 'new normal' would be. Patch and his flock lived across the way, in the main chicken yard with the goats, and Pokey Jr and his chicks lived in this secure and smaller run. All chickens were happy, healthy and living the life that was intended for them.

Summer to Winter

as it seems to do every year, spring led into summer and summer would soon lead into fall. There were changes in the weather, which led to changes in the set up and rhythm of the chicken yard. With each day's bedtime happening later all the chicks were able to stay outside longer. No one seemed to mind as there was more time to scratch and peck. Eat and drink. And dust and sunbathe. There were occasional breaks to play, and of course, to stare into Patch's chicken yard and wonder what life was like over in the big city.

With all their needs met, there was no burning desire to move out of the cool and safe set up they had with Pokey Jr. But young chicks often dream of bigger things. And living with goats, in the main chicken yard, was definitely considered a bigger thing. Every now and then, they were brought back to the reality of the day when Pokey Jr would sound the alert for a predator. That was a great reminder that they had it pretty good where they were.

As they moved towards adolescence, the tail feathers, mannerisms and way that Pokey Jr was shadowed, made it clear that at least two of the chicks were growing up to become roosters. It crossed Pokey Jr's mind that a hostile 'Patch like' takeover may be, again, in his future.

While this run was safe, spacious and a good size for seven chickens it was WAY too small for three roosters and four hens. He didn't worry about it, too much, as they were likely not going to be ROOSTER roosters until next spring. Additionally, he would be older, a bit wearier and perhaps at the right age to move to become a respected elder and advisor to the next generation. If that worked out, time wise, there may not be the need for a hostile takeover.

As the summer advanced, the biggest change in a long time happened. The chicks got larger and the area in the run became pretty barren as all the grass and vegetation had been pecked and scratched away. While this made dust bathing incredibly awesome, it did reduce the adventure of scratching and searching for bugs among the plant life. This was recognized by their chicken keepers and some moveable poultry netting was placed around the run. Pokey Jr, having seen most everything in his many years, understood what was happening and was both anxious and excited. Excited because he realized they would have more room to run, play, hunt for bugs and simply explore. The anxiety appeared as he knew that this benefit was balanced by the increased exposure to predators on the ground, as well as hawks and other aerial threats.

The second wave of excitement and anxiety were different sides of the same thing. Pokey Jr was excited to be able to be a full-time rooster again. It's fine to help your chicks grow and to teach them where treats are, but a rooster's gig is to protect. He would now be able to get back to what he was fully born to do.

But, there was also concern in him as to whether or not he had fully prepared the flock for predators. He had orchestrated occasional warnings signals whenever he spotted danger, and they reacted as they were built to do. But was it enough? And, having not really roostered in over a year, was he still sharp? Was he still an effective leader for the flock, or was he too old and just didn't know it yet?

Pokey Jr's plan, which was well thought out, was to gradually ease them out into the extended run by first keeping them close together. That way, if he spotted a predator and sounded a warning, they were close enough that he could gather them to safety quickly. When he had more confidence, he could ease them out into areas that would take them a bit more time to scurry back to the security of the enclosed chicken run.

But, as life in the chicken yard sometimes does, it moves at its own pace. And when the door flung open, any hope of a slow and gradual transition was lost. The chicks raced around like toddlers coming downstairs on Christmas morning.

Within seconds Pokey Jr transitioned back to lead rooster. His plan was foiled by the pure joy of young chickens, and some switch flipped inside him. He was back with his head up searching the perimeter and sky for any hazards. While it was initially a bit nerve wracking, it was also exhilarating, as this is what roosters are meant to do.

This was how the rest of the summer and early fall went. The only real changes were the growth of the chickens, and the confirmation that Chip and Penguin were, in fact, roosters. All was good, everyone got along and there were no 'real' power struggles. There were the typical rooster games as Chip and Penguin would crouch down with neck feathers flared and would jump chest to chest. There was nothing violent to it and nothing aggressive. It was just the way young roosters practiced, so that when it was time to establish a pecking order, they knew their place. It also allowed them to understand how to use their spurs and to practice developing their protective skills.

Well, there was one other change, once again they had completely torn through all the vegetation and that created a bit of a problem for everything but dust bathing. On hot windy days, the dirt and dust made it difficult to breath, got the water dirty and also wound up in the food bowls.

With the chicken run being a permanent structure, it wasn't going to move. There was only so much space to adjust the poultry netting to provide additional play areas with grass. The real answer was to give this area a rest and allow it to recover. But the only other option, of places to go, was the main chicken yard. Pokey Jr knew that there was a 50/50 chance and wondered how it would go with Patch if he returned with his own little flock to protect.

Through the fall, and into the early stages of winter, the poultry netting was moved a few feet this way and then a few feet that way. This would provide some grass, but it seemed to be torn through within a week and the problem returned.

The temperatures dropped pretty brutally as winter started to show its face. That presented little worry for Pokey Jr, as no molt had happened on any of his chicks this fall. Additionally, with the trees not having leaves, his vision kept him a few steps ahead of any predator attacks.

But one day, the cold did have an interesting impact. When they left the coop in the morning, all their waterers were frozen and there was nothing to drink. Thankfully, the chicken keeper brought out fresh water, but by noon it too had iced over. This went on for a number of days and was confusing for Pokey Jr. He had navigated several winters and couldn't remember water freezing this often. He made sure that whenever fresh water was brought out, he called his flock over, to make sure they stayed hydrated before it would freeze again.

The main chicken yard didn't seem to have this problem. Pokey Jr wondered why it was just his flock that was affected by this. What secret does Patch have to keep their water from freezing? After a bit he spotted it. The waterers in the main chicken yard were all heated and he wondered why his flock did not have the same set up. It was not good for their health and couldn't possibly be fun for the chicken keeper to have to haul out fresh water 2-3 times each day.

Pokey Jr stared at the waterers hoping to crack the code on the heated bases so he could implement it with his flock. When watching them get cleaned, he spotted his answer. They had to be unplugged. A set of extension cords ran the length of the farm and it was likely there wasn't enough cord, or power, for both yards to get heat. Combine that to the lack of vegetation and it was clear to Pokey Jr that they would soon be moving to the main chicken yard.

When chicks get excited, they typically ask the same questions over and over and over again. Pokey Jr decided, for his own peace of mind, to not discuss this potential move with his flock until it was actually time. Until then, he would keep practicing on gathering them together in crisis and keeping them close when free ranging.

He did feel lots of excitement on returning to the chicken yard. Pokey Jr grew up with all of the chickens in there, kept them safe and led them well during his time as lead rooster.

Admittedly, there was some ego at play too. The last any of the flock saw him, he was a beaten, wounded and unemployed rooster. Pokey Jr's return, from the important mission of raising his own flock, would be viewed with great respect.

He was, though, quite anxious to see if Patch would welcome him back. Pokey Jr would be returning with his own small flock and wouldn't be a threat to Patch's leadership. However, and whenever it happens, it was a new adventure and Pokey Jr was ready for it.

Moving to the Big City

The next morning, when Pokey Jr came out of the coop, he saw both the frozen waterer and the frustration on the face of their chicken keeper and knew that today would likely be moving day. His rooster radar went into full engagement and his head darted around to make sure he made eye contact with all of his flock. He made his call to bring them in tighter and the chicks knew something was different. That alone sent them into full obedience mode.

They all dreamed of the move and what living with goats would be like, but each had a different version of how it would all play out. Of course, as chicks, they had dreams of a storybook and romanticized tale. But how it would unfold, none of them could imagine.

It was time. The move to the big city. First, the hens were scooped up one at a time, by the chicken keeper, lifted over the fence and placed in the big chicken yard. Pokeymon was first. She dreamed that the chicken yard would be paved in grubs and mealworms and that everyone was kind and welcoming. What she found was quite different. Everyone looked over at her for a moment and then went back to scratching and pecking without a welcome or even a nod. There were no grubs anywhere to be found and she didn't even know where the food and water was kept. This transition was toughest on her, as she was the first in and had no idea if the rest would join her.

It felt like an eternity, but was probably less than a minute, until Martha was placed next to her. Pokeymon wondered if she had the same bug-eyed look Martha had when she was first placed in the chicken yard. If she did, it was no wonder that no one came to say hello to her. Next, Bumble joined them and shortly after was Clover. With each added chick, the look of panic was lessened, and the look of excitement increased.

However, in their old chicken run, Chip and Penguin were freaking out. While not fully roosters, they had begun the transition to 'protector,' and there is nothing worse for a rooster than to have their flock taken from them. They were in full panic mode. When they were picked up they screeched and squawked in a way that had far less courage behind it than any of the hens' noises. But within seconds, they were also placed in the big chicken yard, and were met with the same relief and excitement that washed over the others.

Last, but not least, was Pokey Jr. His excitement and anxiety were far different than the others. He was SO excited to rejoin his original flock, but he was also very nervous. Would they remember me? Would they welcome me? Would Patch accept him back? Or would he be shunned, attacked and embarrassed before his new flock that viewed him as a king. Soon all these questions would be answered.

Before he could think about it too much, the chicken keeper gently lifted Pokey Jr into the big chicken yard. Without asking any of his flock to stay close, they were glued to his hip. Since a rooster's first job is to watch out for his flock, and since Pokey Jr had a ton of nervous energy, he walked them over to show them where the waterers and feeders were. It was obvious that all the hens recognized him. Some nodded, some smiled and some ran over to say hello.

Pokey was first over, as she was so happy to be able to see and talk to her son again. He, too, was thrilled to see his mom. Gone are the days of ego where having your mother dote on you was embarrassing. Now it was just a moment filled with joy and wings wrapped around one another.

Wherever Pokey went, Sis was soon to follow and she wedged her way into the conversation.

"Oh Pokey, who have we here? Introduce me to this handsome fellow."

While some may say this in jest and others may play along. Pokey knew that Sis was most likely serious and had no idea who Pokey Jr was.

"This is your nephew Pokey Jr." Pokey said.

Sis nodded and stared for a moment as if she had recognized him.

"Well good day to you, sir and welcome to our chicken yard. Very good of you to visit your mother."

Nothing happens in the chicken yard without Patch knowing about it and he was well aware of the new residents.

There really was no malice between Patch and Pokey Jr, it was just the business of being roosters. So, Patch noticed, nodded and went about watching over his large flock and allowing Pokey Jr the freedom to watch over his.

The first day seemed to go well. Pokey Jr took his flock and went to the south side of the chicken yard and Patch and his flock stayed on the north side. Lumpy and Stormy raced over to say hello, as they really missed their buddy, but soon after a quick greeting they returned to the comfort and protection of their flock.

Everything appeared to be working out and that the two flocks and two lead roosters could all coexist. At night Pokey Jr would get his flock all into the same coop and away from Patch. During the day they would split the chicken yard. It all seemed to be going well until Pokey started to hang out more with Pokey Jr and his flock.

That didn't sit well with Patch and he let Pokey know it. Out of respect, she went back to his flock, but would find herself drifting back to her son many times during the day.

Patch let it go for a while but knew that everything in the yard was seen and often gossiped about by the many gossiping hens. He had enough and charged Pokey Jr to let him know he disapproved. Roosters are not easily intimidated, and Pokey Jr was no different. Internally they are wired to be brave and strong, and externally it shows itself as strength and confidence. So when Patch began showing signs of aggression, Pokey Jr didn't back down.

Not only did he not back down, he actually charged at Patch. He didn't draw blood or hurt him but he was clearly a different and more driven rooster than the one Patch kicked out of the chicken yard about a year ago. Pokey Jr knew he had to demonstrate his strength to his new flock and that any show of weakness would create anxiety in them, so he fought. It wasn't what he wanted to do, but it was what he had to do.

It was incredible and may have been a result of the pent up frustration of a rooster that had been unable to be a rooster for a long time. He dominated this encounter and eventually chased Patch into the woods.

Everyone took notice and Pokey Jr's flock was thrilled to see that their leader was the top rooster in the yard. Patch's flock, however, was now in turmoil. They are trained to align themselves with the strongest rooster, for self-preservation, and now they were torn. The rooster that protected them well, a year ago, was back and looked strong and fearless; and the rooster that has bravely protected them over the past year, was looking scared and weak. Who to follow?

Knowing these flocks well, Pokey Jr was locked in on both reactions and was thrilled to be the proud, strong and heroic leader his flock worshipped. But he was also a very wise rooster and was well-aware of the response to Patch. Patch's flock was now split with half wanting to come to rejoin Pokey Jr and half wanting to stay with Patch.

When Pokey Jr saw this reaction he was devastated. As an older and wiser rooster, he understood how it all works. He knew that Patch was the best fit and best leader for the main flock and that he had now divided them. He also knew that he was too old to oversee a flock of thirty. In taking some of the main flock's respect from Patch, he was dooming them.

The Night After the Night Before

inside the coop, Pokey Jr was solidly locked inside his own head and replayed a lot of memories from the past year but soon he began to focus on the last 24 hours.

Having driven Patch into the woods today, Pokey Jr had clearly sent an unintended message to both flocks that he needed to fix. Ideas jumped around his head all night. As much as he hated the solution that he finally landed on, he knew it was the best one, and the one he was driven to make happen.

He also knew that yesterday's fight had taken some confidence from Patch. It had also rippled through the flock and many were now questioning Patch as their leader. There aren't many ways to return confidence to a rooster. In fact, there may only be one way and it was quite a painful one. Roosters are confident when they are the strongest leader available to the flock. Pokey Jr knew that and knew exactly what had to be done.

As the sun was coming up he let out as many massive crows as he could. His goal was to 'appear' to be the biggest and baddest rooster around. Then, when he got his butt kicked by Patch, it would elevate, even more, Patch's standing with the flocks. It was going to be physically and emotionally painful and truly humiliating. It would rip away the confidence of Pokey Jr's flock and worry his mom no end.

Flocks are genetically developed to link with the rooster that can keep them alive and safe. What will happen this morning will have his flock, the group he has raised since they hatched, lose faith and trust in him and imprint on Patch. In the end, it was the best thing for both flocks, the best thing for Patch, but a gut-wrenching reality for Pokey Jr.

Once the coop was open, Pokey Jr headed in the direction of Patch. Immediately Patch ran away, which made Pokey Jr's plan much more difficult than expected. The message he sent Patch yesterday was that he was in charge. So, every move to engage with Patch today was viewed as an aggressive one. He needed a Plan B, as simply rushing towards Patch wasn't going to work. He had to wait to encourage Patch to fight for control of the chicken yard. The problem was Patch wasn't aware there was a plan.

If Pokey Jr's idea was visible to anyone, it wouldn't work. He needed to find out how to engage Patch in a meaningful way. Roosters are driven in a couple of areas–protecting the flock and breeding. So, Pokey Jr felt the next best way to 'engage' Patch would be to make advances on his flock, and that's what he did.

Pokey Jr started to dance for Wanda, one of the loveliest hens in the chicken yard, and a longtime favorite of Patch. Wanda looked at him like he was crazy, as it had been a long time since anyone put the moves on Patch's favorite hen. Initially she thought he had lost his mind and paid him no real attention but when he kept dancing and 'flirting' with her she began to get annoyed.

Patch was witness to the entire event and was caught between two minds. Pokey Jr, as wise as he is, could see that and so he kept dancing. Wanda simply wanted to scratch, peck and eat and just went about her day. But after she was full, she was ready for her morning dust bath and there was no way she was going to jump into the bath with Pokey Jr acting like a crazed lurker. She shot Patch a look that clearly articulated that she was done and would like Patch to address Pokey Jr.

For Patch, instinct took over and he raced to Pokey Jr. Plan B was in action. No one was oblivious as to what was happening. Both flocks were split and confused. In the last two days, they had bounced their loyalties and trust between these two roosters.

Both roosters crouched down, flared out their neck feathers and stared at one another waiting to see who would make the first move.

For Patch, this felt like an all or nothing moment. If he fought and won, he likely regained the trust of his flock and would return to the lead rooster role. However, a loss on the heels of yesterday's loss would be devastating and likely mean the end of his time as head of the flock.

For Pokey Jr there were no 'Ifs' because today's battle would be a loss. He would make sure of it, and in doing so, would banish himself into certain irrelevance for the rest of his days. As monumental of a decision as this was, and as much as it would negatively impact the rest of his days, he had no hesitation in what needed to happen.

It was simple and a decision that we each, I believe, would want to make in a similar circumstance. What's best for me or what's best for the survival of my family and friends? We each would be Pokey Jr in this moment, wouldn't we?

It had to look good, and Pokey Jr knew it, so he threw the first spur. It nearly made contact, but Patch was fast, locked in and able to dodge it. The battle was 'On' and Patch was back to being Patch. Thoughts of yesterday, thoughts of legacy, thoughts of the flock were all out of his mind. Instinct took over and he struck back with spurs flying.

Pokey Jr wasn't 100% sure that he could have dodged this strike if he wanted to, but he made sure that he didn't want to, and took a spur to his comb that immediately drew blood. Combs bleed at an alarming rate and so it immediately looked good for Patch.

Pokey Jr threw back and made sure to make contact so it wouldn't look 'fixed.' In addition to making it look legit, he was still a proud rooster. And while he was willing to lose the trust of his flock, he wasn't willing to completely embarrass himself. The strike made contact, did no real damage, but it did click Patch into the reality that he was in a fight and he doubled down with his focus.

Back-to-back strikes by Patch were followed by both rooster's spurs clicking in mid-air. Adrenaline was flowing full force and neither felt the pain or reality of the immediate moment.

The damage was clearly on Pokey Jr's side with a sliced comb, wattle and gash on his chest, but he felt none of them. The reality of retaking the lead rooster position in the chicken yard was lost on Patch, as he was flying solely on instinct and the desire to win the battle before him.

With blood dripping into his eyes, Pokey Jr realized he'd made it a 'believable' performance, and that he was soon able to end it and have the chicken yard return to a sustainable hierarchy. To fully convince all the hens that Patch was 'The Man,' he knew he needed to take one more strike on an exposed chin, like a boxer on the take. Patch, who was fully connected to the moment, struck and his spurs slashed across Pokey Jr's face.

With the latest strike, the moment was over for Pokey Jr, and he needed to get out before Patch hit him again. While the adrenaline was still pumping hard, the pain had begun to enter his nervous system. He saw Patch readying another strike. Pokey Jr raced to the gate of the chicken yard and turned to look over the kingdom he once led.

Patch was confused at the flight of Pokey Jr and took a moment to collect himself. The rest of the chickens were all staring with mouths agape astonished at what had just happened.

Pokey Jr was debating if jumping the gate was the right move or staying in the yard would be best. It wasn't tough to read everyone, as they all had the same expression.

Within moments it appeared that Patch had made the decision for him. He raced to Pokey Jr to drive him completely out of the chicken yard. Pokey Jr knew that leaving was the right move.

Had he remained, it would have continued to put a strain on Patch's ability to lead, but he knew that leaving would paint him in a really negative light. His legacy as a warrior and a hero was hanging in the balance but so was the long term health of the flock and so he did what heroes do and jumped over the gate, and left the chicken yard and his legacy for good.

Patch took a moment to digest everything. You simply can't have as much at stake as he did and fully just return to a typical day. He was jacked up and it would take a while for him to calm down.

Even though every chicken in the yard had an elevated heart rate, they all seemed to find some level of calm rather quickly. Everyone returned to scratching, pecking, drinking or dust bathing as they were prior to the big showdown.

And as life returned to normal, inside the chicken yard, it moved back to abnormal for Pokey Jr. It was too painful for him to stay just outside the fence and watch them all return to chicken life. Plus, he needed to find a safe place to rest and recover. He in no way wanted that to be within the sight of anyone in the chicken yard.

This devastated Pokey. It was tough to lose a son, especially a good one like Pokey Jr, but it was so gut wrenching to lose that son twice. And with tears in her eyes, she watched her son stagger out of sight.

"*Hey Pokey, whatcha up to?*" Sis said as she noticed Pokey staring out of the chicken yard.

Too tired and emotionally drained to even reply, she just shook her head as Sis moved on to scratch and peck nearby.

There was only one place Pokey Jr knew of that was out of the sight, safe and secure, and had food and water. Albeit cat food, it was still calories and would help him in his recovery.

With that, he used the rest of his energy to get himself to the back porch and up on his bucket. Here he was able to calm down and look over the beating he just took.

The chicken keepers recognized his condition and immediately came to his aid. While this was comforting and appreciated, it was also tough to accept, as it likely meant the end to ever being a real rooster.

Back on the Back Porch

The return to the back porch was humiliating. Pokey Jr never doubted that it was the right thing to do, but that didn't lessen the fact that he was a completely irrelevant rooster in the world of chickens. His legacy, his impact on the planet, and his memory in the minds of every chicken that knew him was– nothing, zero. This was a difficult place, for a once proud rooster, to be.

Normally a rooster falls at the feet of a predator and is remembered as a glorious warrior, OR they age, and are replaced by a younger rooster that they have mentored. Neither of these options were available to Pokey Jr. He had to live with the reality of being a rooster in his prime that wasn't good enough to oversee the flock and rule the chicken yard.

Now, living on the back porch all alone, there was nothing to distract him from these haunting thoughts. Pokey Jr had no desire to continue to live. Every day was filled with the memory of what he was and what he should be.

Even though the farm was big, most of it was visible to the chicken yard, and he found it very difficult to be in any place where he could see the life that he was supposed to live. He knew it was Patch's time to look over the flock. But it was still a painful reminder, so he chose to not put himself in a position where he could see that life was going on just fine without him.

Sadly, or happily, depending on how you look at it, he had started to bond with the chicken keepers. He would get first crack at leftovers. Be fed both first in the morning and last at night. Got extra treats. And had daily massages of his legs and under his wings. While all this was great, it still wasn't how a rooster was supposed to live, and he knew it.

His days and nights were, technically, not lonely as he had human companionship. Pokey Jr knew it wasn't the right path for a rooster, however, it was the right path for him. It provided love and companionship, and at the end of every day, that was really a very good thing for him.

He actually began to enjoy the smiles, joy and comfort that he would bring to his chicken keeper, as well as his family and friends. Perhaps his destiny wasn't to protect and guard chickens, but maybe it was to help a human accept, and stop struggling with, the reality and path they were on. For who knew better about taking a different path than Pokey Jr.

Having gone through all he had gone through, he was perfectly equipped to help others who were struggling with relevance and purpose in their lives.

As days moved forward and months rolled into one another, Pokey Jr and his chicken keeper both took comfort in this very unique interspecies relationship that appeared to work very well for both of them.

If this was the best life had to offer, a rooster without a flock, then it was still a good life. Pokey Jr was grateful and embraced it. Until one day in March when, once again, he overheard the talk of incubation and hatching.

Was it possible? Would it be happening again? Could anyone even conceive of a second, second chance?

Regardless of what each day may bring, this was enough to give Pokey Jr hope. The possibility of once again helping a group of chicks grow and learn how to survive in the big crazy world was an enormous rush of adrenaline.

If life held nothing more than being best friends with his chicken keeper, well that was fine too. He was going to provide comfort and guidance to a chicken keeper or a flock of chicks. Either way he is a happy rooster once again.

After all, Pokey Jr did get to enjoy many unique journeys with his chicken keeper. Going for coffee together at the local coffee shop became a regular activity. Additionally, rides around town or sitting in a custom made sidecar on the tractor were pretty cool moments too. And every now and then, he even got to go inside and enjoy a soccer game or two on TV.

In the end, Pokey Jr's legacy as a proud rooster and best friend to his chicken keeper is not bad and really all any rooster could ask for!

Brad Hauter

Brad Hauter

Brad Hauter

Epilogue

Currently the chicken yard dynamics are similar to what is articulated in this book with one, recent, exception. We had a predator attack, in Patch's yard, as this book was heading to the publisher and Patch was missing with two hens from his flock. Two days later he returned missing feathers and with some deep scratches. We are nursing him back to health but the experience has certainly toppled his reign in the chicken yard.

He now spends most of the day in the corner, as Pokey Jr did, and Beaks (our crossbeak rooster) appears to have taken over the top spot in the flock... It is still very recent and very fluid so... We shall see.

Afterword

This is an interesting book to me as it really wrote itself. The adventures, conflicts and successes played out before my eyes.

The uniqueness of what I was witnessing gave me hope and inspired me that second chances happen if we keep living and never give up.

What I Learned from watching this dynamic I felt important to share with a wider audience. I hope you find as much joy and fun in reading this as I experienced living it.

About the Author

Brad Hauter is the men's soccer coach at DePauw University and host of the TV show Coop Dreams. In addition, he is a budding homesteader and best friend of Pokey Jr!

Follow, like and subscribe to Coop Dreams on -

Coop Dreams Facebook - https://www.facebook.com/coopdreams/
Coop Dreams Instagram - https://www.instagram.com/coopdreamstv/
Coop Dreams Twitter - https://twitter.com/coopdreamstv
Coop Dreams YouTube - https://www.youtube.com/channel/UCEdbn
NQ61o4OFZWxJlhTZgw

Coop Dreams APP

To watch episodes and see more of Pokey Jr download the FREE
Coop Dreams APP

FREE for iPhone and Android
Mobile viewing of Season 1-6!

Go to the Apple store or Google Play
and search Coop Dreams

Watch the Coop Dreams channel on Roku and Amazon Fire

Printed in the United States
By Bookmasters